PLINY

AND OTHER PROBLEMS

EMILY FERNANDEZ

LOS ANGELES † NEW YORK † LONDON † MELBOURNE

Pliny and Other Problems by Emily Fernandez

ISBN: 978-1-947240-84-1 Paperback

ISBN: 978-1-947240-85-8 eBook

Copyright © 2023 Emily Fernandez. All rights reserved.

First Printing 2023

Cover art by Dennis Callaci

Layout and design by Mark Givens

For information:

Bamboo Dart Press

chapbooks@bamboodartpress.com

Bamboo Dart Press 040

www.pelekinesis.com

www.bamboodartpress.com

SHRiMPER
www.shrimperrecords.com

In honor of Pliny this book is

"…written for the masses,
for the farmers and workers,
and to interest people in their leisure time."

Contents

Please begin 6

Problems

Ode to Boredom 8
The Compliment 10
Echo of the Heart 11
A Serious Case of Jazz Hands 14
Fabric 15
Midnight in Quarantine 17
Lucky Lady 18
The Manspread 19
Cool 20
In the Lurch
    (or Waiting for a Reply to my Email) 21
The Marriage Table 22
The Spiders You Swallow in Your Sleep 23
The Trees 25
Sorry, No Apocalypse 26
Battleground 27

Pliny

The Peonies 30
Women Facts 32
Fire Within 33

Prodigal Musing 35
Pliny 36

Supplications

Questions from Below 39
The Lifeguards 40
Liquefaction
    (or A Spiny Mole Crab Appears at the
    End of the Pandemic) 42
Gillnet 44
The Pacific Ocean 45
at Bruce's Beach 46
Glacial 48
Flash Flood 49
Tapestry 50
The Master 51
Resurrection Moss 52
Lost Garden 54
Snow Dreams 55
Sky Above Clouds IV 56
Supplications 58

Epilogue

Victory 61

Please begin

Please begin
Please open your eyes
place your feet on cool tiles
Please walk through doorways
Please take your first sip of coffee
Please remember to look at the elm tree
Please see how many roses bloomed
and how many weeds have gone to seed.
Please remember that today is not yesterday,
that sleep is meant to divide us from the past,
and night is made to give us thought space.
Please know that clock hands neither hold
nor strangle you in the present moment, but
they will scoot you along one minute to the next.
Please do not pretend to know the future, but
keep a calendar and a journal all the same;
It's only fun to climb if you have a song to sing.
Please forget everything I just said
Please splash water on your face
Please stretch your bones
Please eat a strawberry
Please breathe deep
Please let love in
Please begin.

PROBLEMS

Ode to Boredom

We were lukewarm lovers once
on the first floor of a tenement building
on the edge of Somewhere.
You sat with me for hours
and listened to my complaints.
I openly hated your smirk,
your still eyes glaring at me
while I watched raindrops
crawl down windowpanes,
or the blinding sun slip
behind the bare hills.
But at least when I screamed,
you echoed back. You licked
my tears with your tired tongue.
And now I miss you
want to be pulled into your vacuum.
You offered me flowers, I remember now.
And warm blankets, empty oceans,
and long, meandering thought.
You created a large shelter
in small spaces of time,
cuddled me with your promise
of the doze and sigh.
But I pushed your leaden arm off
and ran headlong toward the sound
of screeching bats and ticking clocks

and thunder. I scream now
and my voice is lost in a thousand others.
It never comes back.
On this steamrolling train
between some here and a little there,
I long for you. I long to lie on the couch;
while you sit, far too comfortable,
on the wooden chair, and admire,
as you always did,
the shape and suck of my yawn.

The Compliment

I might snatch it from you

like a yellow craven troll might
take a locket from your neck,
crawl on feet and fists to his cave,
open his gnarled fingers,
marvel at its possibilities.
He might try it on,
stare at himself in the murky,
moonlit waters. He'd doubt
the image for sure,
be dazzled by the sparkle,
measure all else against it,
open it up, and see
that it contains
nothing.
He'd throw it,
stumble back upon it,
lose it, want it back.
It would become exhausting!

But even with all of this
I have yet to say
I'd want to do without it.

Echo of the Heart

Know your pain.

We grasp at such truths;
the clumsy metal claw
in an arcade game.

By the time I self-diagnosed:
stress; a knot so tender
in my back, it sent shocks
through my chest,

I had spent nights
contemplating the world sans me,
the mess I'd leave behind.

It started with the question:

What was I worth?

The article, "Women Don't Act
at First Symptoms of Attack,"

and all that rejection, too.

I called my doctor,
the appointments made.
Who could ignore the spondee
"Chest pain?"

So I panted on the treadmill,
braless, wires connected.
She said "Keep looking at the flowers
or you'll faint"
as the Chinese peonies throbbed
with each rushed breath.

I lay half naked
on the crinkling paper
the cold wand pressed under breast
revealing the shadows
flashes of fire — reds and orange —
violet blue specks on the screen

as the whack-back of my beat,
my sound unmuted, saturated
the room.

Twice they saw deviations in the EKG,
an awkward hill, a flattened valley,
but nothing amounting to death.

Know thyself.
 Know thy pain.

How often we cannot
though we feel its intimacy
burn within.

How often stress
makes voodoo dolls of us.
The brain consumes
the body,

Plays its games –
Perpetrator/victim –

until blindfolded
we are bluffed.

A Serious Case of Jazz Hands

For Gina

You thought you were cured.
It had been hard for so long.
There were no predictions
in the weather or bird signs.
Just the same old same,
the flatline of possibility,
that expected maturation of the soul.

And then the arrival of your loves
seemingly unexpected
because you forgot how to anticipate.
The booze was a probable cause, too.
And the onslaught of memories
in the beat and rhythm.
It spread like a virus through
your midlife veins, itching you
through and through, a fever too.
The heat and flush of laughter.

Only this can explain the video:
You dancing outside in the dark
to the Pointer Sisters
hands fanned out like peacocks
hips shaking you sick with silly.

Fabric

I watch our dark clothes spinning
together – shirts, pants, boxers, bras,
nothing delicate – and I am dazed
because another family I admired,
unraveled. And I can't but wonder
if a timer is ticking on my own?

My sons' jerseys and *Jurassic World*
shirts, my now-too-tight jeans,
my husband's grey button-downs —
for suits he's wearing more these days —
tumble upon each other like a blur
of time-lapsed clock hands, and
when I see this on a dusk evening
sitting on a plastic bench
in the stillness of the empty
laundry mat (because our machine
is broken), anxiety hits me like wet
towels, and I think maybe I've been too
happy for too long. Or negligent.
Or cruel. And it gets tangled
like the knots of frayed hems,
and I realize I don't know how to be
tender like I was when folding
newborn's clothes. Each onesie
held to my nose, fragrant as fresh fruit.

You get to an age when
you can't get the stains out,
the wrinkles stay, and you are left
with this single desperate hope
that when you pull your family's
warm laundry from the dryer,
it will still feel like love.

Midnight in Quarantine

The coyote has long since gone
but the old pit bull still barks
at the edge of the chain link fence
for hours without pause.
I lie in the dark and wish
for soothing birdsongs but then
quickly remember the screech
of peacocks or the macaw,
and find a little comfort in the runt's
guttural response; an echo
of my nature, the things I can't
let go of that I know are already gone
the way we all stand in the pitch dark
bodies tense on the dew-soaked lawn
until we know of nothing but
our hearts that yammer on
like a dulling meditation
some kind of soulful elegy
for all that has gone wrong.

Lucky Lady

When I was nineteen
my balding boss,
an Italian restaurateur,
told me to eat my self-bought meal
with him during my unpaid break.

He announced
"When I die,
I hope it is on top
of a woman."

"Lucky lady,"
I said, and put down
my fork while
he ate his calamari,
which I later found out

was pig's bung.

The Manspread

Today I want to sit like a man
knees wide open, push my gut out
let my arms lie limply beside me
like dead fish.

I'm tired of the helicopter
circling above like a whip.
For hours it searches,
a panting, hungry beast,
while the criminal nestles in,
takes a nap under someone's
backyard trash heap.

Today I want to eat like a man
shove shit in my mouth
unbuckle my belt, let my soft flesh
protrude like an uncooked ham.
I'm trying to get some satisfaction,
that's all.

I like to cross my legs in tight jeans,
most of the time. But there are days
when I'm as tough as the rest of them
greedy, with grit in my teeth,
when the bad drivers and cop chopper
twist my underwear in knots,
and the man in me wants to fuck it all,
fuck it all.

Cool

When I was twelve, a friend
held me underwater.
It wasn't cool: the bubbles
in my eyes, hand hard on my neck,
the whipping of my tangled hair
and the blast of "Don't You Want Me"
from her pink radio cutting
through the water in my ears
as I finally gasped for air.

I was invited there to play
in her swimming pool.
No one was around, just her father's
pigeons crammed in their cage,
beady eyes, beaks bobbing through
shadow and the shit-stained wire,
as she laughed and carried on,
but they must have known
that she almost killed me.

The rest of the visit I remained
untouched though some of me
was still held under, and all
I knew was I had to get away
yet had no choice but stay.
I was almost thirteen, gripping the lip
of the pool, wearing my first
string bikini, trying to act cool.

In the Lurch
(or Waiting for a Reply to my Email)

Am I now to be your butler,
down upon my knees, waiting
patiently for your arbitrary ring?

Black like ash from a burnt-out
fire seeps into the sags
under these sleepless eyes.

I've become a beastly mismatch
of graveyard hopes rashly plucked
then dashed like dying flowers.

I'd rip out the second-hand muscle
that pumps the blood now reeking
of my rotting anticipation

all for a nod of love or recognition!
But you slice past me like a skiff
on a vast and placid lake.

Oh! I am merely mist that you
stare through, squinting those eyes
into impenetrable slits.

So focused you are,
even your ears have silenced
the shrieks of my beseeching!

What do you see, oh Master?
What could possibly be more pressing
than my monstrous countenance?

The Marriage Table

> "Not all dreams need to be realized."
> —Patti Smith

The kitchen's florescent light illuminates
the threadbare curtains. At the wooden table
old as my childhood, stained
and nicked, we reminisce, cradle
our warm beers, pull from our worn canvas hearts
the dreams that have fallen to the bottom.
We packed them away when we thought
they were broken, when we couldn't
figure out how they worked,
when they reminded us
of our failure. In our rambling buzz
we examine them for new purposes
and admit that time has made them
silly. And we start to laugh
again. This I know: we must not toss
them in the trash bin. Let their impossibilities
become the batteries (if only) to energize
this new moon night, this one shared lifetime.

The Spiders You Swallow in Your Sleep

Often my mouth is wide
open: a welcome mat that reads
everyone and everything

I buzz with yes
feel the vibrations
like new wings
pulling the universe closer.

My mind and muscles
hail me as their owner.

And then I lose a little sleep.
And a little more. My smile
starts to sag. My feet
want to hang out to dry,
and the calendar
has no space to breathe.

In my sleep
I start to swallow
spiders.

And they are hangry
biting me up inside
swelling my ankles and eye bags
until I must ice them,
sitting like a broken boxer

while I drink coffee
and avoid the plan for the day.

Tangled in their web,
my mind chokes on the gauze
and my muscles mutiny.
Cover me in your cocoon,
I cry, hide me from my welcomed
guests. Do me in.

But like all creatures,
they eventually die away
and I fall back to the ground.

Stretch a little.
Clear away the cobwebs
and the clutter.

I open my eyes and mouth,
singing again the season
of butterflies.

The Trees

what we imagined
were perennial weeds
we let grow into mangy
little trees with roots
too deep

trying to pull them
up with our bare
hands would've taken
everything in us

so we gave in, let them
grow thick trunks devouring
chicken wire fences

roots lifting the concrete
of our foundation

until we become jungle.

our house slowly
disappearing into an obscenely
natural state

until our neighbors complain
of our love gone wild

we screech like abandoned
parrots in our tangle
of branches and leaves.

Sorry, No Apocalypse

New Year's Day 2017

The decorations hang from the rafters
waiting to catch fire and drop ash on us,
the wasted and weary, clasping our fingers
but the bright paper flowers will not have closure,
only collect dust, shiver slightly in the breeze,
slowly fade to grey.

We are tired of talking about the apocalypse,
we have nothing more to prep, beyond ready,
we've stopped lighting candles
or burning incense and sage.
We are on our knees, pleading,
with old clothes, and stories, old wants
and needs – a little justice, no more tyranny –
but there will not be a burning sky
nor a voice from above striking us
with a tongue through our hearts.
We wait for the new year holding our breath
with blue lips and red eyes.
We look at each other with our faces
drooping from our skulls like skin we need to lose.
Waiting.

Someone will have to break the knife
on the bread gone stale, drink the bitter wine,
laugh our way back to love and struggle again
in this same old stupid world.

Battleground

How do you approach
the battleground where you lost?
The ashes are cold. Flowers now bloom
between the black bones of broken trees.
Why even go back? Better to let the grass
grow over the blood of ghosts.
But we all go back.

Do bodies crave pain? Or maybe
we want to find the hope that was lost
when the shrieking fell to its silence.
Its echo follows us like a feral dog
barking at our heels. Maybe we need
to return the echo, give it a proper burial.
And what is a proper burial? How many veils
do you need? How big must the tombstone be?
And how do you stop it from being exhumed,
a scar ripped open like a mouth?

How do you return
to the battleground where you lost?

Do you go alone, late at night,
under a sky so cloudy, stars can't
shine through with their piercing eyes
of possibility? Do you go with lovers,
their arms around your waist,
holding you up in the hot sun

just so you can tear away
from them, their support a suffocation?

Maybe you shouldn't.

Maybe you must. Go there, fall on your knees,
take the soft ash in your hands, you must.
Rub it into your eyes, cake it on your cheeks.
Let your tears carve new paths
on a face that has turn to stone.
However you choose,
                                      you must.

PLINY

The Peonies

> "They recommend us to uproot [peonies] at night-time, because the woodpecker of Mars, should he see the act, will attack the eyes in its defence."
> —Pliny the Elder, *Natural History*

When my red roses burst into full bloom,
I know what is to follow. Within a week
I'll down my second glass of wine alone,
grab a serrated knife to saw the deadheads off
while the fireworks of the feral teens
blast the suburban scene.
It'll be dusk when my skin snags on thorns,
and I curse the bush and remember the lure
of flowers, and her naïve request for peonies.

How they fall apart in such a mess
like young women with their first-broken hearts.

You went into the forest with your old friend Pliny,
notebook in his hand and quill behind his ear,
to dig up a bare-root tuber to surprise your love.
It was just like you to want the bush,
not settle for them cut and vased,
only to droop upon her bedroom vanity.

The woodpecker told old Pliny
not to touch his peonies,
yet you both proceeded in unheeded.

You for the love of her,
and him for the love
of the larger experiment.

You shoved your hands into the spongy dirt,
and pulled up the root, bloated and twisted
like the hand of a miscreant.
How you must have thought that your love
would last, that she would still be around,
when the leaves and flowers grew.

But her heart was secretly with the Elder.
And to make matters worse,
when you squinted into the glistening sky
pouring through the trees, that brutal bird
swooped down and pecked out your eyes
with his jarring rapidity.

The blood dripped around your feet,
much like these brittle petals will surely fall
in this heavy summer heat.

Women Facts

> "hailstorms, they say, whirlwinds, and lightning even, will be scared away by a woman uncovering her body while her monthly courses are upon her."
>
> "if a woman strips herself naked while she is menstruating, and walks round a field of wheat, the caterpillars, worms, beetles...will fall from off the ears of corn."
>
> —Pliny the Elder, *Natural History*

Woman cries out in the hailstorm
Blood rages within like a whirlwind
A body, naked, illuminates in lightning

Letting loose the ancient shame.

At sight of her:
Caterpillars see their future wings.
Worms know the fecund depths.
Beetles feel the vibrations of their song

And have no shame.

Fall from the ears of corn.
Return the queen to her hive!
Hide your frightened men.
Women will call them out

And feel no shame.

Fire Within

> "In all fables we are told That the Salamander is born in the fire"
>
> —The Book of Lambspring
>
> "This animal is so intensely cold as to extinguish fire by its contact, in the same way as ice does."
>
> —Pliny the Elder, *Natural History*
>
> "One-third of the planet's amphibian species are threatened with extinction."
>
> —U.S. Geological Society

They worried about the salamander going extinct
but salamanders don't go down like that, baby!

Pliny threw them into the fire, just to see
if they were ice cold. Sure, walking on water
is cool, but what about walking on fire?
What about putting it out with just a touch?
Being born from flame? What about the myths
saying you are a magician, you are a glowing tongue
of light, spitting poison, killing off a thousand troops
by bathing in wine? What about dipping yourself
in honey, putting us in the mood for love, or death?

Oh, drench me in that salamander blood!
I want to know what it is like to not fear
the heat that is ripping through the world.

To be that cool when wildfire burns down
a mountain range that circles my city,
and ash drops like snow, and we choke
on thick air that turns our daylight orange.
Choke on the IPCC reports, put our hands up
to the decades of waiting for the myths
of deniers to finally lose their steam.

Pliny was disappointed to find that, in fact,
the salamander *died* in the fire, disappointed
like the naturalists who know, all too well,
extinction has it out for even the coolest of us.

Prodigal Musing

> "a town in Spain was undermined by rabbits"
>> —Pliny the Elder, Chap. 43. "Nations That Have Been Exterminated by Animals." *Natural History*

They prefer my dew-soaked greens.
I prefer the spoils of their fecundity.

Let them destroy the exotic plants.
They can pillage the gardens, too.

I like that. I like to keep the game
alive. The gardener exhausts himself:

traps and cats and vegetable cages
while wild ones dart in every which way.

We have wool coats buttoned to the neck,
a castle erect. My room is empty and cold.

They warm together in the dark of their caves,
tussle in the dirt and dried leaves.

These rabbits keep coming and coming,
bring cousins and predators in an orgy of play.

Let them take from me these tender leaves
Let them be brutal in beguiling ways.

---

*poem also based on "Young Boy Feeding Rabbits," by John Bradley (USA, b. England) 1831

Pliny

"Hastening then to the place [Mount Vesuvius] from whence others fled with the utmost terror, [Pliny the Elder] steered his course direct to the point of danger, and with so much calmness and presence of mind...He was now so close to the mountain that the cinders, which grew thicker and hotter the nearer he approached...Here he stopped to consider whether he should turn back again; to which the pilot advising him, 'Fortune,' said he, 'favours the brave.'"

—Pliny the Younger *(on his uncle's death)*

"Laocoön...a work that may be looked upon as preferable to any other production of the art of painting or of statuary."

—Pliny the Elder

his lover speaks:

I watched you hold true
to your love. My malodorous
doubt must have sweat
through the pores
in my pits and along my brow
as I uttered, "Yes!
I believe in you.
Yes."

But my funk didn't matter.
Nothing did, except this:
we were on a ship heading

toward the belching volcano,
so you could breathe
in Fortune's breath.

The pupils in your eyes tighten;
your smile stretched.
You turned to make love,
but not to me. To some
dream, some furnace inside
you bursting forth. Unstoppable,
at least by me, my feeble grip
around your wrist.

Had I known! The veins
that my fingertips kissed
would soon stop pulsing,
the viscous air burning
your lungs like lava.
You were alone, by then,
under the rain of rock.

When we found you
your hand had fallen off;
one way to break my clasp
I guess. Covered in ash,
your agony looked like the
cut marble of an ancient
Roman figure fighting
his serpentine fate.

SUPPLICATIONS

Questions from Below

Is it okay to feel so little
to not shine very bright
to simmer
to shut your eyes
but not sleep
let the morning sun
fracture in the trees
color the backs of your
eyelids a golden red,
indecipherable shapes,
and not ask what it is?
Why does it seem
like an art form
to feel so little
to not ask much?
Like when I was a girl
in the ocean, I'd sink
to the sandy floor
let the rumbling tumble
of a giant wave
pass over me,
as my body lay flat,
still as a sand dollar,
only slightly pulled, and
then I'd rise to the top
breathless, exalted in
seafoam and sunlight.

The Lifeguards

The low tide pulled its blanket
off the edge of the shore
and showed its crabs and shells.

I walked to the place under the pier
where weekly I go to watch the waves
crash along the concrete pillars.

I bring my questions. Learn to listen.
Ask "what next" and "what to do"
about the little pains that plague me

Today the water seemed so shallow,
and a thin shaft of light beamed through.
The waves spoke gently, "we're safe."

What if I kept walking through the pillars
to where the long shadow ends
and the ocean is pure and blue?

I steadied my feet, feeling for the sandbars
that lifted me up to my ankles or dropped
me into waist deep pools of green.

Like a ship to the sirens, I followed
my song — risk hardly real. Just me
wading through the watery hallway

of the cathedral — to exhalation! –
until I heard the whistle shrill, breaking
the magic of my trance.

I am a lifeguard's worst nightmare
and this was not my first time they
called me back or chased me to the shore.

An amateur open water swimmer,
at 45, I decided I could swim out past wild
breakers to the playground of dolphins.

Sometimes when you love something
you are willing to go neck deep
in the thing that can kill you in a minute.

Sometimes you are just fucking stupid
walking through pillars knifed with indigo
barnacles in the rush of erratic waves.

The lifeguard stood in his red shorts
reminding me of my dumb human frailty
and his required need to care for it.

I turned quick at the whistle's sound
suddenly shamed as I sloshed back
toward my audience of beachgoers.

On the dry sand, I pretended to listen
to the lifeguard tell me what I already
knew. Then, I walked back to my chair

a half mile away — picking up sand dollars
that snagged the glassy shore — giddy
with an idiot's grin I could feel in my ribs.

Liquefaction
(or A Spiny Mole Crab Appears at the End of the Pandemic)

Sand sucks the body in. Ten legs
quicken like wings, liquify hard
surfaces, to disappear in a snap.

Some creatures don't fret breathing.
Not like us. We all seem
to be gasping these days.

One of my students wanted to bury
herself. I said only if you learn
to breath in dirt. Not really.

I wrote, I see you, just like I said,
I see you to the spiny mole crab
that appeared at my feet.

But my student is online.
I have never seen her, and
barely saw the mole crab.

It was above ground briefly
moving its giant sand crab body
to a shallow wave, digging in again.

My student says that her words
are not worthy. My soul sinks. Who
is *not* remarkable in this world?

I searched that night to learn more
about the creature and read only
classifications and brief descriptions

nothing about the way I felt, seeing it,
no mythical story to match the magic,
the wonder wrapped within the moment.

Same when I read my student's words,
her brilliant delight in nature, or the
darker turn: to end her remarkable life.

How much of her voice is holed-in,
trapped in an idea? I call the care team,
and it takes my breath away.

If you jump in the swash zone too long,
you create your own quicksand.
I want to pull my students out of that.

I want them to know that survival
will not always be a battle, that we
can lean back, shake loose our legs,

roll out of it like sand crabs –
write ourselves into presence,
ready ourselves for the remarkable.

Gillnet

> *According to the WWF: "The vaquita is the most endangered cetacean in the world"*

Diamond-shaped, open-mouthed
drunk on sea water, the nets abound.
Some are tied to the lovers of the catch

and some move like ghosts, like virus
still weighted, they wait for the unwitting
indiscriminate as American bullets.

This microfilament nylon moves
casually, not a lure of seduction,
but hiding in plain sight, catching
bodies. Soon the vaquitas may vanish.
If you didn't know this, the news snags
on your gills and leaves you tangled.

Round-eyed porpoise, bystander in
the crosshairs of commerce, ensnared
below the surface of the Sea of Cortez.

The Pacific Ocean

Between Santa Catalina Island and San Pedro, I had a window seat. The ocean stretched to the horizon. Because I had been on vacation and had become accustomed to amazement, I hoped for something wild. A shark or dolphin swimming alongside us, a seal, a school of fish, or mermaids.

For a long while I didn't see so much as another boat.

I wanted to be the person who shouted out "there" like when I was looking for orcas on a cruise along the Washington/Canada border. Even though the cetaceans were far away we all moaned with delight at the slightest flash of a fin. I wanted it to be like that, all of the passengers gathered at the window with fingers pointed at the wonders of the world.

But this coastal stretch of the Pacific offered nothing.

And I thought "oh this is what hopelessness feels like." The long reach of water, the empty feeling that drops 3,000 feet deep. Luckily, on the Catalina Express, I knew there was some life between me and the ocean floor. Others had told me so. Moray eels, angel sharks and giant sea bass amid a tangled kelp forest. "And so, this is how faith works," I thought. This is knowing beyond seeing. This is being human in ordinary times: open to the imagination

in the face of infinite blue.

at Bruce's Beach
for Ada

not far off along the shore
a Black woman walks
with measured step

her sandals dangle
from her finger, a thin scarf
hangs upon her shoulders

long braids sway
behind her silhouette
tangle in the wind

the sun shines through
glassy turquoise waves
catching her gaze.

She stops, faces the sea
it rushes to her ankles,
anchors her in sand.

She looks past the breakers
to the horizon, then
her head tilts back

until all she can see
is the expanse of the sky.
She opens her arms

and owns it.

* *It's been almost 100 years since the city of Manhattan Beach, an ocean-side community outside of Los Angeles, seized Bruce's Beach from the Black couple who owned it. Historical documents proved the act was perpetuated by racism, and last year the city returned the property to the couple's descendants.*

—Theara Coleman "The Story Behind Bruce's Beach" *The Week*

Self portrait by Adaeze Anyanwu

Glacial

Warming water chisels the glacier
with Michelangelo precision.
Each wave crashing creates curves
and caves in the body.

After my friend was murdered:
an iceberg calving from the Ronne Ice Shelf
big as Belgium slides into the ocean.
A monstrous crack.

For my mother,
still alive but slowly gutted by dementia:
a slow melt, small waves lapping
the edges. Sculpting my ambiguous
loss with Arctic grief.

Flash Flood
for Carol

A tree topples like the news
of your passing.

The valley howls.
Leaves gust like ghosts.
My hair might blow away.

How could I have known
it'd be our last call?

I stand at a cliff's edge.
It tells the same story:
one step too many, there's always
the rock bed, rough water below.

Knees brace for the downpour.
It slicks the bridges,
rivers the roads.

There's no such thing as burying
you, claiming higher ground.

I hug the branch within my reach,
leaves in my teeth. The river swells.
The mudslide drags even worms
from their dark slumber.

I hang on until it gives way
to a deeper canyon floor.

Tapestry

I've been craving this poem for days,
staring at a wall stained with memory
of dead vines. The sun cuts small cracks
through spring clouds.

                      My mandarin tree
grew a thick branch of sour grapefruit,
my yellow miniature rosebush bursts with
loose magenta blooms, the donut peaches
are now shaped like teardrops. By accident,
I know how to grow a bitter pumpkin,
a spiny squash.

Montaigne says that nothing is pure.
Even this melancholy covers me in a
tapestry of watercolor wisteria, and
buried in the cloth are real seeds. A bee
thinks my ear is a flower. I think I cannot
stay the same much longer.

                      Cross pollination,
hybridity, adaptation, call it what you will.
I light the match, hold it to the candle wick
just to feel the hiss of transfer and flare.
Where does the wax go? Into air.

The Master

On the first hot day in LA
I poured some coffee
and headed to the deck.

On a chair I propped
my winter legs
and let the sun glare.

The dove and crow
sang their song
in a flourish of elm leaves,

and then a fly lighted
on my knee. A few
others came and went

but this one stayed
rubbing front legs,
hind legs, in ritual —

the green iridescence
the grey web of wings,
the touch so delicate.

We are in quarantine
together in the new
warmth on Earth Day.

Do this, the master
whispered. Move lightly,
one body on another.

Resurrection Moss

Considered dead, you are
a tawny clump of dried twigs
on dusty rock. But within
your leathery bones
is a body rolled inward
in prolonged meditation
absent of tears or sweat,
thought to be victim
of prolific sun and cracked
river beds, you are asleep
for the long haul,
teaching us the virtues
of paralysis.

A kind of magic sugar
working miracles
with salts to outlast
a sustained longing
for soft mist to kiss the soil
and seep to root.

After the first rains,
long into the new year,
you will turn your open sign
bright green, your
wiry arms outstretched
to a world that withers

in the heat of its desire
teaching us the surprise
of survival.

Lost Garden

Buried here, the dead roots of a dwarf avocado tree.
Once the size of our baby,
it grew tall enough to make small fruit,
enough hope to make us stay —

but as we remodeled,
the branches turned to sticks by a drought (and neglect)
and the young bodies of children turned to men —
once they swayed on a rainbow hammock
hung between two citrus trees
torn down for a concrete patio,
where I sit at sunrise, hear ghosts of chickens,
while my dogs sniff the burial ground
remembering how their jaws
bloodied the feathered necks and closed translucent lids.

These old songs skip like worn out records —
that time I held the lens close to tiny green tomatoes
and chili peppers still wearing their brown flower skirts
and the seedlings of spinach sprouting, already pocked
with holes from hungry loopers.
The first egg held in a toddler's fist.

The elm tree that did survive
grew defiantly through a chain-link fence
stretching skyward,
leaving long shadows over wild invisible things, unframed.

Snow Dreams

The temperature 100 and rising
on the long drive up the 5,
through the dry throat of California.
The only views: a thousand golden
low-rolling hills, speckled with
scrawny oaks, an occasional industrial farm
with its hypnotic rows of almonds and grapes,
the faded half-moon on the left,
sun beating through the windshield.

An hour past the capitol's
thirsty mouth, into the drooling
delta, a strange vision hovers
low in the distance,
a snow-capped mountain
glowing pale orange and hazy
from the ashy air of another
raging fire further east.

Shasta's singular icy peak
shimmers otherworldly:
a chunk of the moon
broken off, fallen to earth,

reminding me to stay the course,
that this world will eventually
rise up before me with quenching
beauty, though fevered it may be.

Sky Above Clouds IV
> *for Georgia*

At twenty I felt the wet emptiness of a cloud.
I wanted it to be a *thing* I entered,
but the air around the enormous balloon
simply turned thick with mist. No tangible
cloudness. Yet I stood in the basket, looking down,
and saw how this *no-thing* thing could be real
enough to make Earth momentarily disappear.

Still, I pretend like things are solid all the time
like the ovals that line the bottom of the canvas.
In the deep blue, each white shape
is thick with paint. They are distinct selves.
None touch the other. Cartoon clouds
that even she could not have possibly believed.

Clouds have never lived up to such
objectification. They have no center,
no stillness, no permanent edges
to draw dark lines around.

But it was the sky above it all
that O'Keeffe was actually after.

The clouds slowly start to shrink
as you move your eyes up the canvas.
They cram in like a wall of rock,
the blue ever blurring into a horizon,

lightening, disappearing, blocking
all view of the ground below,
no leaf of grass, no desert bones
and above, no sun at the end of the horizon,
just its left-over light, its pink haze,
its last promise of day.

Did she make peace with death,
that first time flying in an airplane,
at seventy, looking out at this?

I felt myself dissolving when I was twenty,
and yet I knew that above the cloud
was simply not-cloud, the eternity of sky
and below was green and gravity.
Today I am learning how things can actually
disappear and that this body is not who I am,
not fully, not forever. Just form and unform,
merging into you and floating out of me.

Supplications

Let the white sage ravage our hillsides, and
the jimson weed hallucinate along the paths,
unmolested. Tell the buckwheat it's beautiful.
Water its brittle florets with your tears. Let
the squirrels squander the black walnuts
among the monkeyflowers. Cheer the coyote
making love to gopher holes, head first.
Get drunk with the blue elderberry, bush
sunflower, and seepwillow at the creek while
the red-tail hawk and American kestrel wage
a riot in our skies. The orb weavers will
cloak you in their delicate scarves, and
the darklings will beg you to get down
on your knees to kiss the holy dirt. Abide.

EPILOGUE

Victory

> "forget your underwear we're free"
> —Allen Ginsberg

You stumble
while laughing
limping to a round
of margaritas, dripping
wet in a cathedral, barefoot
in a river of snakes coiling
around your dance like waves
that knock you to knees and crack
to pieces memories of iridescent
abalone shells, and mosquitoes
hum on shoulders as you sing
canticles to the Tanzanian wolf
who couldn't outlive the glow-
in-the-dark African springhare,
(it haunts you in your sweetest
nightmares) as you sleep-swing
in the crocheted hammock, given
to you by a nurse who forgot
the word medicine but scoops
ice cream into palms. You lick
it up as sunset flames the sky,
and the leaves – burnt to ash
by the encroaching fire –
drop around you
like confetti.

Acknowledgments

"Ode to Boredom" and "The Compliment" published in
Exit 23 ZZyZx Writerz.

"Echo of the Heart" published in *The Angel City Review*.

"Midnight in Quarantine" published in *Pangyrus* with a
short essay about the poem.

"In the Lurch" published in *Spectrum*.

"Sorry, No Apology" and "Battleground" published in The
Altadena Poetry Review.

"Prodigal Musings" published in *Ekphrastic Review:
Writing Challenges*.

"Pliny" published in my first book *Procession of Martyrs* by
Finishing Line Press.

"Please begin" and "The Master" published in *The Dewdrop*.

"Resurrection Moss" as "Spikemoss" published in *Black Fork
Review*.

"Supplications" published in *PCC Spotlight Magazine*.

Thank you Mark Givens and Dennis Callaci from Bamboo Dart Press. You have been so wonderful throughout this process.

Thank you Juanita E. Mantz for helping me through the birth of this book.

Thank you to the Pasadena City College English Division and Creative Writing Department. Thank you especially to Kathy Kottaras, Akilah Brown, Simona Supekar, and Kirsten Ogden.

Thank you to Kathy, my office mate, who listens to all of it.

Thank you to all my students.

Thank you to all the women I wrote with during the Las Lunas Locas days.

Thank you to Karineh for providing space for my words.

Thank you to Kimberly and the ZZyZx WriterZ for introducing me to a poetry community in Los Angeles.

Thank you to my early Creative Writing professors Susan Straight and Judy Kronenfeld.

Thank you to Michelle Brittan Rosado, Tim Hatch, Luivette Resto, and Cati Porter for your words.

Thank you to my dear friends Liz, St Jon, Gina, Tina, Amy, Kristi, Maya, Angel, and Alejandra.

Thank you to the people at Dolores Mission and the Catholic Worker Hospitality Kitchen.

Thank you to my beach crew.

Thank you to my loving parents, my sister and brothers, my cousin Amy, and all my family.

Thank you to my loves: Gabe, Agustin, and Joaquin who love me despite my moods.

About the Author

Emily Fernandez is an Assistant Professor of English at Pasadena City College and the author of the chapbook *Procession of Martyrs* (Finishing Line Press, 2018). Her poems have been published in *SHIFT*, *Antithesis Journal*, *Black Fork Review*, *Pangyrus*, *The Dewdrop*, *Angel City Review*, *Tiny Seed Journal* and others. She lives in El Sereno, an eastside neighborhood in Los Angeles, with her family, and she spends her Saturday mornings at the beach. She writes, teaches, prays, protests, and tends to her loved ones, animals, and plants. She does none of this with much patience or grace, but she is still learning.

112 N. Harvard Ave. #65
Claremont, CA 91711
chapbooks@bamboodartpress.com
www.bamboodartpress.com

www.ingramcontent.com/pod-product-compliance
Lightning Source LLC
Chambersburg PA
CBHW080942040426
42444CB00015B/3418